Contents

What is a family?

Families come in all shapes and sizes.
A family can be just two people living
together.

Parents and children, grandparents,
uncles and aunts can all be part of one
big family.

What do we think about

Break-Up?

...an Powell

HODDER
Wayland

an imprint of Hodder Children's Books

Titles in the series

What do we think about …

Adoption	**Disability**
Alcohol	**Drugs**
Bullying	**Family Break-Up**
Death	**Our Environment**

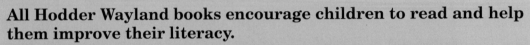

All Hodder Wayland books encourage children to read and help them improve their literacy.

✓ The contents page, page numbers, headings and index help locate specific pieces of information.

✓ The glossary reinforces alphabetic knowledge and extends vocabulary.

✓ The further information section suggests other books dealing with the same subject.

✓ Find out more about how this book is specifically relevant to the National Literacy Strategy on page 31.

Editors: Carron Brown and Kim Protheroe
Consultant: John Bennett, a Health Education Co-ordinator
Cover designer: Jan Sterling
Designer: Jean Wheeler
Photo stylist: Gina Brown
Production controller: Carol Titchener

First published in 1998 by Wayland Publishers Limited
First published in paperback in 2001 by Hodder Wayland,
an imprint of Hodder Children's Books
© Hodder Wayland 1998

British Library Cataloguing in Publication Data
Powell, Jillian
What do we think about family break-up?
1. Divorce – Juvenile literature.
I. Title II. Family break-up
306.8'9

ISBN 0 7502 3251 X

Picture acknowledgements
All photographs by Martyn F. Chillmaid. The photographer and the publisher would like to thank all the people who acted out the scenes and assisted with the photography in this book.

Printed and bound by Eurografica in Vincenza, Italy

Families aren't just about people living together. They are about people loving and caring for each other.

Why do families break up?

Sometimes families break up when one parent leaves the family to live somewhere else. This happens when parents decide they do not want to live together any more.

It may be because they are not getting on together and they have a lot of rows. One parent may have met someone else they want to live with.

What happens when families break up?

When families break up, it can be upsetting and worrying for everyone in the family.

Before they split up, Tom's parents used to row a lot. Tom could hear them shouting at each other when he was trying to get to sleep.

Sometimes, he heard them crying. It made him feel very frightened and upset.

Can you stop families breaking up?

Sometimes it can feel as if it's your fault if your family breaks up. You try extra hard to be good, but you can't change things.

Leah's mum was always telling her off for leaving her bedroom untidy. Her mum said it made a lot of extra work for her.

When Leah's mum left home, Leah blamed herself. Really, it was because things had gone wrong between her mum and dad.

Can anyone else help your parents?

Sometimes when parents are not getting on together, they try to get help. They go to see someone who will listen and let them talk about their problems.

They may still decide to break up.

If they divorce, they will no longer be married to each other. But they will go on being your parents.

Who can you talk to?

If your family breaks up, you will have a lot of questions about what is going to happen and what it means for you. You may feel upset and angry, or just very sad.

Try to talk to someone close to you, like a grandparent or a good friend. Talking it over can't change things, but it can help you feel better.

Where will you live?

If your parents break up, you will probably live with one parent. Your parents can decide which of them you will live with.

If they can't decide, they will go to court to let a judge decide.

When Holly's mum and dad split up, Holly carried on living with her mum. But she sees her dad at weekends and she spends some of the school holidays with him.

Can you see both your parents?

You may be afraid that you won't be able to see your mum or dad if he or she leaves home. Try to tell your parents how you feel.

You should be able to spend time with both your parents. You can keep in touch by writing or talking on the telephone.

You don't have to choose between your parents. You can go on loving both of them.

How will things change?

When families break up, there can be a lot of changes. You may have to move house and live in a new place.

Sometimes, it means moving to a smaller house or flat than the one you used to live in.

You may have to go to a different school.
At first, it can be hard getting used to all
the changes.

How will life be the same?

Even if your parents break up, you will still be able to stay in touch with the people you love, like your grandparents.

You will still have your friends, and the things you like doing together.

What is a stepfamily?

Stepfamilies are like other families, but they are made up from two families. If your mum or dad gets married again, you will have a stepdad or stepmum.

A step-parent won't take the place of your own mum and dad, but you can still be friends with them and get on well together.

When Holly's dad got married again, Holly had a stepmum, a stepbrother and a stepsister.

Holly wasn't happy at first. She didn't want to share her room with her stepsister. But now, Holly and Emily have fun playing together.

What will life be like in the future?

It can be very hard going through a family break-up and all the changes it brings. It can take time to accept what is happening.

But in time you will get used to all the changes. There may even be some things you like better about your new life.

Notes for parents and teachers

Read this book with children one to one or in groups. Ask the children what they think a family is. Try to include examples of as many types of family as possible: lone parent, single child, extended families, stepfamilies.

Ask the children to think of examples of happy family times, and sad family times. Suggestions for happy times could include birthdays, weddings and holidays. Sad times could include deaths and funerals, losing a pet, arguments and family break-up.

Talk about parents' relationships in the context of other relationships/friendships. Ask the children what happens when a friendship breaks up – how people stop talking to one another, or say things to hurt each other, or go off and make a relationship with someone else. The children should understand that, like children, when adults argue they can say silly or hurtful things because they are upset and angry.

Talk about rows and the feelings they bring out in people (anger, hurt, sadness, spitefulness, violence). Get the children to act out a role-play situation of two people arguing, and one or more trying to intervene. Ask the actors what feelings they had when they were arguing, or trying to stop the argument.

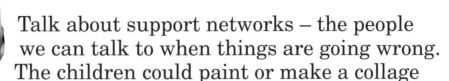

Talk about support networks – the people we can talk to when things are going wrong. The children could paint or make a collage of a tree with roots and leaves. They can label the roots as all the people who have given them support and love in the past (include parents or carers, grandparents, teachers, friends) and the leaves as all the people who give them support and love now. The children should know that there is a continuity of love and support, even if a parent leaves home.

Ask the children if they understand what separation and divorce mean. They should know that divorce is not accepted by some cultures and religions. You can also talk about how the statistics for divorce have changed – that it did not happen so often in the past.

Ask the children if they know what remarriage and stepfamilies mean. They may have stereotypical ideas (e.g. wicked stepmothers from fairy tales) and it will help if you can give positive examples and talk to children who live happily in stepfamilies.

If a child is going through family break-up, they should be encouraged to express their feelings and fears. Routine in other parts of his or her life can be a help in this time of change.

Glossary

Court The place where a judge makes decisions.

Divorce When two people end their marriage.

Judge A person in a court who has to decide who is right when there is a quarrel.

Stepdad A mum's new partner.

Stepmum A dad's new partner.

Stepbrother
A brother in
a stepfamily.

Stepsister
A sister in
a stepfamily.

Further information

Books to read

Dealing with Family Break-Up by Kate Haycock (Wayland, 1995)
How do I feel about My Parents' Divorce? by Julia Cole (Watts, 1996)
My Two Families by Althea Braithwaite (A C Black, 1996)
We're Talking About Divorce by Anne Charlish (Wayland, 1997)

Organizations to contact:

Childline
Royal Mail Building
Studd Street
London N1 0QW
Tel: 0171 239 1000
Helpline: 0800 1111 (Freephone)

National Family Mediation
9 Tavistock Place
London WC1H 9SN
Tel: 0171 383 5993

National Council for
One-Parent Families
255 Kentish Town Road
London NW5 2LX
Tel: 0171 267 1361

National Stepfamily Association
Chapel House
18 Hatton Place
London EC1N 8RU
Tel: 0171 209 2460

Relate National
Herbert Gray College
Little Church Street
Rugby CV21 3AP
Tel: 01788 573 241

Use this book for teaching literacy

This book can help you in the literacy hour in the following ways:

- ✓ Children can discuss the themes and link them to their own experiences of family break-up.

- ✓ They can discuss the characters and speculate about how they might behave in each situation.

- ✓ They can compare this book with other stories about family break-up to show how similar information can be presented in different ways.

- ✓ They can try rewriting some of the situations described in the form of a story.

Index